Building Strong Relationships

And Facing The Challenges

by

Andre L. Ponder

Bloomington, IN   Milton Keynes, UK

authorHOUSE®

AuthorHouse™
1663 Liberty Drive, Suite 200
Bloomington, IN 47403
www.authorhouse.com
Phone: 1-800-839-8640

AuthorHouse™ UK Ltd.
500 Avebury Boulevard
Central Milton Keynes, MK9 2BE
www.authorhouse.co.uk
Phone: 08001974150

First published by AuthorHouse 3/20/2007

ISBN: 978-1-4259-5637-0 (sc)

Printed in the United States of America
Bloomington, Indiana

This book is printed on acid-free paper.

Table of Contents

Introduction

"Building Strong Relationships and Facing the Challenges"

"Building Strong Relationships and Facing the Challenges" is a book of knowledge from the mind of Andre' Ponder. This book is easy to read and understand; written in terms of a counseling session, addressing the mind of the reader by giving suggestions and comments on various issues that relate to building strong and positive relationships with others. Whether the person is a family member, friend or associate all relationships can be nurtured. The Bible gives us our direct foundation for addressing these issues, and any situation that is beyond your control should be addressed to your personal spiritual leader or a professional. At the conclusion of each chapter, the reader is encouraged to generate comments, concerns and feedback and email them directly to the author at the following email address: andreponder@hotmail.com. Each comment is then personally answered and returned to the reader as a follow-up.

Here is a sample of what you might see as a follow-up.

Dear Elder A': In the Chapter - "<u>You did it again</u>" - If concerns and thoughts have been expressed and well communicated (more than once), and the receiving party seemed to have listened and cared, but nothing has changed. Should the person with the concern express their feelings again? *Anonymous Sister*

Elder A': Hello my sister. When it comes to real friendships, a true friend never gives up. They just become more creative or specific in communicating their concerns.

Remember to never allow your need for the other person to change, overshadow your friendship. Some people require a little more time and effort. The key here, is that they listened and cared. *"That's what friends are for."*

Expecting Perfection

As a child, it is sometimes hard to find the right words to say when others challenge you, so we say the first thing that comes to our mind. Paul states in *I Corinthians 13:11, "When I was a child, I used to speak like a child, think like a child, reason like a child; when I became a man, I did away with childish things."* This same biblical principle holds true for relationships. We can't just say or do the first thing that comes to our mind; therefore, as an adult we must learn how to deal with certain issues in a respectful manner.

Consider this as the first question.

"What happens when we allow the countless expectations from

ourselves and others affect the way we live and perform?"

This entraps you in a world of human perfection, living your life through the eyes of others. How many times have you looked into the mirror today? Did you do anything after you looked? What were you looking for? Of course a mirror is still a mirror. This leads to vanity.

"I do not necessarily agree; I would not consider myself as vain."

Let's face it, vanity is simply the way you see yourself and how others perceive you. Still think you are perfect? Try not washing your face or body, combing your hair, brushing your teeth or using the restroom just for one week. Now look in that same mirror, are you still perfect? Does it really matter what other people think of us, or is our own self-gratification all we need?

As humans, "We fall down, but we get up," "We hurt, but we heal," "We stumble, but we keep walking." Sometimes the expectations we set for ourselves and others is far too great, and as we grow, we understand this more. Imagine being a child whose life and actions are expected to meet or exceed their parent's expectations. Can this child really become the person that they would like to be or simply the genius that their parents perceive them to be? We must learn to let go a little, and accept the fact that we too have made and will make mistakes. "When you have done your best, what more can you do?" Stop living your life through the eyes of others and allow room for mistakes. No one is perfect, but the Father. The only way you can keep from making a mistake, is to do nothing.

With that being the case, Christians should never face the public, but live as hermits by isolating themselves from any public appearances.

Think of it this way, "A person who is overly concerned with perfection, should never get married, nor date; they are only asking for trouble."

For the person that is timidly shy, a public embarrassment is too much to handle. Let's face it again, a strong sense of humor helps to relieve the humiliation and shame of any situation.

Consider these.

Can a singer ever hit an off note or forget a lyric? - Just ask any of the greats.

Can a writer ever erase? - Just ask any author.

Can a parent ever make a mistake? - Just ask one.

They Love Me, They Love Me Not

I Corinthians 13:13 "...but the greatest of these is love."

And the second is like it, 'YOU SHALL LOVE YOUR NEIGHBOR AS YOURSELF.' Matthew 22:39

Have you ever walked along picked up a flower and played this game? Hoping that the last petal of the flower would land on, "They Love Me." Well, this is not a game when it comes to relationships. You should always feel confident that he or she loves you. Never allow conditions and circumstances to dictate or challenge your love and commitment to a relationship. Learn to deal with issues individually. Never allow them to affect the love you have for one another. If love is the issue, deal with it. If finances are the issue, deal with them. If communication is the issue, deal with that. (Reading the chapter, "Can We Talk" might help.)

What happens when these things are done and you still need to know?

If you still need to know, than you don't really know if the other person really loves you. It's like this, "Isn't it better to hear, "I Love You" than to ask "Do You Love Me?" This peace and contentment comes from within, it's just something you know. Its like how do you know when you are really in love, you just know it. On the other hand, never assume anything. Assumptions usually lead to issues that need attention. Actions speak louder than words and if you are not receiving any (actions that is, not things) then you had better re-check yourself and the relationship. Start by reading the 13th Chapter of Corinthians.

How do you re-check yourself?

This is done by conducting a self evaluation of what you are contributing to the relationship. Not measuring who does more or how often something is done, but by evaluating what you know to be important in the relationship. Remember, that people are different and perhaps you are more of the loving type. Some people have to be taught how to love. By communicating, they will know what it takes to love you. Follow-up by reading the chapter, "Can We Talk."

No matter how much love you are giving, you can't make anyone love you back. You have to start by loving yourself, first.

I Want My Old Life Back

Sometimes even in the best of relationships, you may wonder if you were better off before this person came into your life; sometimes thinking that you just want out. When you feel this way, read *John 15:4-10*.

Can I go back to the way my life was before I met this person?

Why would you want to do this? Is this relationship complicating your life?

It's known that people come into our lives at different times for many different reasons. We have to learn to choose when and how far to allow someone into our personal space. Never give away any part of yourself that you will regret or want to take back later, including your feelings and money. Allow yourself to experience the developmental stages of the relationship before you just give it all away. Give a person the opportunity to get to know you, rather than reading you from the cover. A good book must be read to be enjoyed, not just thumbed through. Isn't your life more interesting than any good book?

That's deep.

You can never actually go back to the way things use to be. When things happen, they have just happened. Ever spilled any milk? Cleaning the milk up, does not change the fact that the milk was spilled. When this happens, we become a bit more careful hoping to prevent the milk from spilling again.

Look at it this way. Once a child is born, some mothers experience post partum depression and perhaps wished they had never had a child, but when these feelings pass, mom is just as happy as the child. On another note, have you ever been promoted or given a greater responsibility? How did you feel when you first started? Not so good, right, but once you got the hang of things, there was no turning back. Consider what the word of God says, *"No one, after putting his hand to the plow and looking back, is fit for the kingdom of God." Luke 9:62.*

Um!

Remember this also. "For better - for worse, for richer – for poorer, in sickness – in health, until death us do part." Some thing's are forever.

I'm Mad With You

How dare you! Do you really think no one else can notice when you are angry with someone?

We choose those who we think it's ok to become angry with. Ask yourself this question? Is my anger management consistent with everyone I know? Would I act this way in front of my spiritual advisor, my doctor, my child's principal, my parent, my neighbor, a waiter in a restaurant, a police officer who has just pulled you over, or just in front of the people we think that may not mind seeing us act this way? Strangely enough, the consequences of acting this way in front of an arresting officer could land you in jail or leaving with a really big ticket to pay. Now think, which is more important? To nurture a lasting relationship with people we come into contact with each day or prove to an arresting officer that you have everything under control?

This leads me to think that sometimes we take each other for granted by allowing ourselves to become angry. On another note, what if that's the last time you saw that person again? Would you really care about the last run-in you had with them or do you really care about that person? Life is short within itself and there are no guarantees. Learn to try and live each day to its fullest extent without having such short fusses.

So are you telling me I should never become angry?

Not at all, anger is a condition that is usually imposed, unless you are just an angry person, and this could lead to a self-esteem problem.

What does self-esteem have to do with anything?

A lot, sometimes it's too high.

Most of the time we become angry because someone did something that **we** did not like, and **we** felt the right thing to do was to become upset.

O.K.!

Try this approach, don't allow yourself to become angry the next time something happens that you don't like and watch the other person's response. They'll become shocked to notice that there is a change in your behavior and in most cases will smile to know that you are now getting things in control. The Bible makes this plain, *"Do not be eager in your heart to be angry, For anger resides in the bosom of fools." Ecclesiastes 7:9.*

Becoming a born-again Christian is just that, you are now re-born and things that use to get you upset and uptight no longer affect you the same way. People are constantly reading your life as a Christian, and it's more important to show it than to say it.

More Blessed Than You

What does this mean? Does it mean that you have more money than the other person, or that you are better looking, a little smarter or better yet, you drive a better car. Strangely enough many perceive this to be just that. A relationship should not be contingent upon who can contribute the most or seems to have things more in perspective. We must remember that by the grace of God we are who we are and without him, we are nothing. He is the one that makes everything possible, and the fastest way to ruin any relationship is to think more highly of yourself than you should.

It should not matter, who paid the last time or whose car you decide to drive. Strong enduring relationships require a lot of give and take, and sometimes you have to give more. That does not mean that you are anymore blessed than the other person, only that you are in a better position for the time being. With this being the case, consider how you would feel if the roles instantly were reversed. So what if you have more money, are better looking, smarter or even drive a better car. All is vanity and when it comes time to leave this life, you can't take any of those things with you. Learn to share and not to compare your blessings. *"Remember that the earth is the LORD'S, and all it contains, The world, and those who dwell in it." Psalms 24:1.*

Ties That Bind

Be committed and know that nothing will tare the relationship apart. This requires a combination of a few of the topics discussed in the previous chapters and some to follow. Here are a few of these suggestions.

Communication – Talk and share ideas on what and how you feel. Tell each other, "I Love You." It's that simple.

Trust – Never get this confused with love, a lack of trust can lead to a lack of love. Don't challenge every issue.

Honesty – Say and show what you really mean, don't hide the truth.

Keep it simple – Don't over exaggerate any situation or condition.

Justifying – Don't justify all your actions, leave room for improvement and learn how to give and accept constructive criticism.

Time – Find time for your relationship. It's not a given. Cherish every moment.

Sharing – Learn to share everything, even your loved ones. You are not the only one that loves this person. There were other people in their life before you came along.

Prayer – Pray for each other.

Knowledge – Get to really know each other.

Lighten up – Leave room for errors and growth.

Flexibility – Be open to change, break the routine.

Team work – Become team players.

Counsel – Seek only good advice. Avoid bad connections.

Apologies – Say and show that you're sorry.

What Makes You An Expert?

I'm often challenged with this question. I'd like to answer by saying, "Ingredients." Ever had a good pot of soup, a delicious slice of cake, or some good bar-be-que sauce. There's your answer.

You still did not answer my question, be more specific. I mean in giving advice.

Now you're talking. Experiences, not theories have taught me how to capture the necessary elements of any situation and to make them better. Sharing thoughts is all I do and you can do the same, that's what this book is all about. Start now by sharing your thoughts, you too will become the same expert. Consider this, "You don't have to be an expert to provide meaningful advice to the choices that people make."

For example, just think of anyone who has ever had to deal with a difficult situation. Consider all the positives of that circumstance that made you a better person.

Nothing about it may have seemed positive to me.

You're reading this book, right. That's positive. Now share your survival techniques that brought you through.

It's not the fact that you went through an ordeal, but it's what and how you did things that make you an expert.

Remember that Prayer is the key and faith unlocks the door. *"Trust in the LORD with all your heart and do not lean on your own understanding. In all your ways acknowledge Him, and He will make your paths straight." Proverbs 3: 5, 6*

You Did It Again

"How much more can I take?", "I can't take this any more!", "I don't have to take this from you!", "Why do you keep doing this to me?", "Here we go again!" Ever hear these or think of these phrases?

These would be good statements and questions to ask the enemy as he constantly tries our faith, but do we really understand why things continue to happen. Let's face it, the enemies job is to steal, kill and destroy. Not just once, but on a regular basis. Do you find this to be a reality?

Yes, but I'm not dealing with the enemy now, It's my _____ ___.

Why is it that we can accept what the enemy does constantly, but when it's our _____ _____ we have trouble finding space to forgive for the same offenses?

Does that mean we have to just fall victim to what ever people do to us consistently and just take it?

Offenses will come, this is a guarantee. No, you don't have to just take it like that, but take it to the Lord in prayer and tell him and the other person how it makes you feel when they do this to you. If this person really loves you, then allow them to commit to not purposely hurting you again. This is a defense that could salvage and nurture your relationship with that person. Think about how important this person is in your life, can you afford to loose anyone as close to you? That sounds fair, doesn't it? Therefore, you should take the necessary actions to preserve any relationship that seems to be on an emotional see-saw. Acceptance of others is better than trying to change them. This takes us to the next chapter, "When Sorry Isn't Good Enough."

When Sorry Isn't Good Enough

Sometimes saying, "I'm sorry" isn't good enough, but "Apology not accepted, nor If you are so sorry, than you would not have done it," should ever be the case. When in doubt, re-read "Expecting Perfection."

You deserve the best from any relationship, and when sorry isn't good enough, allow the agreement to include flowers or lunch. You make the stake. Try this, "I've forgiven you this time, but next time it will cost you a teddy bear and a bottle of perfume." Real loving relationships will not block out such commitments, but would make the other individual more conscious of his or her actions when it comes to similar offenses.

I'm smiling now, this might work.

Remember men like rewards also. It's not always their fault. I say this because most men are a little less likely to share how they really feel.

Why is this?

You'll have to write in for this answer.

When offenses are done purposely, knowingly and intending to hurt, then that is a bigger problem. God has equipped each Christian with such attributes as love and forgiveness, but he never intended for anyone to become a door mat for pain. *We are also commanded to pray for those who persecute us. Matthew 5:44.* This will help, but when it's gone too far, professional and spiritual counseling is suggested.

Is That What You Really Mean

Who ever said that loosing your cool, was cool? There is nothing cool about it. Emotional actions as a result of anger should never be intended to hurt or upset the other person. Your actions should only demonstrate how you are feeling. So what if you are not as close anymore or it does not seem like you are friends anymore. Does this give you a right to go into your bag and spread gossip? It is very immature and untrusting for you to do this when you are upset. Just because you are angry with this person, why would you want others to feel the same? I guess the old saying, "Misery loves company," stands true in this case. It's wrong! When your feelings have changed about a person, keep them to yourself, don't become a lose cannon of information. Allow yourself to heal in the best way possible without destroying the character of the other person.

What if they were wrong and it wasn't your fault?

It does not matter whose fault it is, two wrongs don't make it right. Calling a person names, insulting them or responding with demeaning and belittling behavior never won any battles or preserved any friendships. Such actions cause a person to consider, "Is that what you really mean?" There are some actions and words that can never be taken back, once gone out they can never be retrieved. This is a good time to read or re-read the chapter, "When Sorry Isn't Good Enough."

Well, I was angry.

There is also the chapter titled, "I'm Mad With You," that will address this issue.

Outside Influences

Try hard to keep all negative outside influences out of any relationship. The Bible clearly states that, *"Bad company corrupts good morals." 1 Corinthians 15:33.* Nothing is more wrong than to accept unwise counsel and outside looking in is always a different view.

It's ok to seek advice for support, but when the advice given becomes detrimental to a relationship that only needs a little tender loving care, than the wrong type of advice could lead to a relationships demise.

Try changing **"outside influences"** to **"inside influences."**

What does this mean?

It means that two individuals should try and resolve their own issues collectively by any means necessary. If things get to the point where you need a third party, try and choose someone that you both have confidence in. A person that you both trust not to take either person's side is always a plus. Deciding whom to choose should be a collective effort.

Keep in mind that not all outside influences are bad, just be careful. You would not want to share anything with a person who would become totally shocked with the information you are sharing with them about the other person, especially if they also know them. They may view them as being wonderful, but when you are finished, this may taint the way they now see them.

Consider your intentions. Are they to help or to hurt? Learn not to add fuel to a fire by telling the wrong person. Certainly you would agree that not everyone has your best interest at heart.

Can We Talk?

Communication is the key and a strong foundation to any lasting relationship, without it you have nothing to stand on. Communication within a relationship can also be viewed as the highs and lows of any situation. Can we talk, should not be a choice, it's a must. You have to talk to make any relationship stronger; however, not verbally all the time.

This makes it easier for men, because it is believed men aren't the perfect communicators and that most women always want to know what is on their mind. A blank look or stare does not always mean something is on your mind, it's simply a look. Answer this, "What does something on your mind, resemble on your face?" How does it appear, and why is this asked so often?

Is this because women like to talk?

Talking is not always the best way to communicate. You should practice more creative ways of communicating and watch the response you receive. When things are done differently, it allows the reciprocator not to become use to your routine. For example, don't ask for a kiss, just do it. Don't ask, "What would you like to eat," know his or her favorites and prepare them.

This sounds like too much work.

A builder never built anything without working and the Bible says *that if anyone is not willing to work, then he should not eat. 2 Thessalonians 3:10.* So if you don't work at communicating, how do you expect to eat of its rewards?

No one is a mind reader, don't leave others to guess what's on your mind, share your thoughts and the things you like and don't like. When you communicate effectively, this leaves little room for error of interpretation on anyone's behalf.

You will find that most problems aren't really problems when you communicate.

Life Is Too Short

Ever wish you could do things over? There is one thing in life that is sure, and that is death. We don't like to talk about it, but we should. Ever think about when or how you will leave this life or your relationship? We will never know; therefore we should cherish the amount of time we have with each other while we are still here.

Choose your battles carefully. Not every issue should be addressed with such tension and debate. If you feel that a conversation or situation is headed towards a certain dead-end, avoid it. Learn to love without such sensitivity and attention to detail.

Does that mean that you should brush things under the rug?

Not at all, just avoid things that lead to destruction. Requiring a person to dot every (**i**) and to cross every (**t**) is not necessary in any relationship. "Expecting Perfection" gives more insight on this matter. Also walking around with a chip on your shoulder isn't good either, eventually it will fall off.

Life has a way of just passing us by without even noticing it. Imagine holding a beautiful butterfly in your hand and once you've touched it, it just vanished away. Life is like that, once we have been touched by someone, thy too, just like the butterfly will soon vanish away. Therefore it is suggested that we make the best of any relationship and hold on to the positive things that they bring, for soon it too will pass away.

Let's Work Together – We Need Each Other

The process of building a relationship requires effort from both individuals. You have to work together and make this a team effort. Ever played tug-of-war? Even though there is resistance on both sides, there is still team work. Try to build and work as a team within your relationship. Think about what would you be without this person in your life?

What if you feel you are giving more, and "Who is really in charge?"

When it comes to giving more, it may be that you are really receiving less. Learn to make the best of any situation and not always feel you should get something in return for your efforts. Remember that the Bible tells us, *"It's more blessed to give than to receive." Acts 20:35.* Therefore, when we give with the intent of getting something in return, this defeats the purpose of giving. Just keep giving and good will come back to you, this is your gift and it is also your reward.

To address who really is in charge? No one is. The only divine order established is; **God – Man – Woman – Children.** Try changing this order and see what you get. Being in charge does not mean being the boss or a dictator either. Respect in any relationship is earned and not demanded. If you have to remind others that you are in charge, then you are not really in charge. Learn to work together to create a balance.

Can't We Just Get Married

This is a topic that I am sure will hit home for many couples deciding whether or not they should get married. Think about these questions first and list your answers on a separate piece of paper.

1. What's stopping you?
2. Are you really ready?
3. Is the coast clear?

Let's address these issues separately.

What's stopping you? What are some of the barriers that are preventing you from just doing it now? Answer these questions in there entirety.

- Have you prayed about this?
- Does this person really love you?
- Do you really love this person?
- Does this person have a job, and what are their spending and budgeting habits?
- Do you share the same spiritual beliefs on marriage?
- Are they available? Are there children involved; is there an ex-spouse or an old relationship they are still holding on to?
- What's their family history like?

These are just a few valid questions, that when answered can be very beneficial to any relationship. Obviously something is stopping you from getting married if you're not married yet. Find out the facts first, marriage is not one of those things that you want to rush. It is a spiritual bond that should not be entered into lightly. I can write a book on this subject alone.

If a person does not have a job, what can they really do for the relationship? Relationships require money, and in most cases, the value of both parties together is far greater than what one person can do alone.

If you have to ask yourself constantly if this person really loves you, then you had better start re-thinking the idea of marriage. Yes, they may love you, but is love enough? This would be a good time to read the chapter, "They Love Me, They Love Me Not." Know this, "If a person really wants to marry you, you would not have to ask them, they will ask you."

Note: Men don't always pop the question first.

Sharing the same spiritual beliefs are important, but what are they concerning marriage. You need to know the other persons stance on divorce as well. Just saying you are Christian does not exempt you from becoming another statistic.

Are they available? This may sound like a far fetched idea, but it's important to know. Never allow yourself to fall in love with someone you can't have.

But what if it just happens and you can't help it?

That's an excuse and not a real good one. Things don't just happen, in such a case; you have allowed them to happen. The Bible instructs us not to covet anything that belongs to our neighbors. Again, we can go on and on with this subject, please write in for more information.

Maybe you are or maybe you are not ready, but is your partner really ready? When the time is right, you will know; however, don't let this time be based upon your biological clock or your desire to just have a man or woman in your life.

Building Strong Relationships and Facing the Challenges is a simple easy to read book that reveals the truth about relationship issues. It was created by Andre Ponder to help deal with the difficult decisions of what to do when faced with a relationship matter.

Written in terms of a counseling session, each chapter is very short and takes only minutes to read, but its unique insight based upon God's word that can last a lifetime.

Whether the person is a family member, friend or associate, this book suggests that all relationships can be nurtured. At the conclusion of each chapter, the reader is encouraged to generate comments, concerns and feedback and email them directly to the author. Each comment is then personally answered and returned to the reader as a follow-up.

Contact Page

For a follow-up, send email to:

<u>andreponder@hotmail.com</u>

Subject line: Book Information

Chapter: _____**Title:** _____

Dear Andre': _____

_____

_____

_____

_____

_____

_____

_____

_____

_____

_____

_____

About the Author

As part of the human race, relationships are being formed at the time of conception. Whether it is with a parent, friend, sibling, teacher or co-worker, all relationships require effort from everyone involved. From the time that I was a little boy going through adolescence, puberty and maturing into an adult, my experiences helped me to understand the importance of building strong relationships with those who really matter.

Not all relationships are productive, some are even counter productive. Personally having to deal with the elements of both forms, this gave me the initiative to share my experiences and reactions as they relate to God's word, "The Holy Bible."

As a youth minister and mentor, I have learned to share thoughts, opinions and ideas on a variety of relationship issues, signifying through God's word, that we can conquer the negative challenges of relations and make them positive. Remembering that, *"All things work together for good to those who love God, to those who are called according to his purpose." Romans 8:28*

Born in Fort Lauderdale, Florida, Andre' Ponder is a gifted singer/songwriter, choir director, youth minister and now author. As an aspiring performer, he has formed his own gospel ensemble that has blessed many across the nation.

Elder "A" as many know him, has taken his talent a step further by appearing in various TV/Film and Commercial Extra Roles.

As a songwriter, Andre' has written the national theme song for the United Church of God, Florida and his music has been featured as a promotional theme song for the National Baptist Convention. He is now prepared to address such issues as "Expecting Perfection" and "When Sorry Isn't Good Enough" as they relate to building strong and positive relationships.